THE EPISTLES OF JAMES, PETER, AND JUDE

Christian Living Bible Study Series

by Trina Bresser Matous

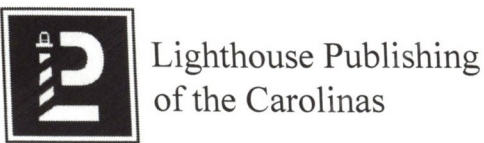

Lighthouse Publishing
of the Carolinas

THE EPISTLES OF JAMES, PETER, AND JUDE BY TRINA BRESSER MATOUS
Published by Lighthouse Publishing of the Carolinas
2333 Barton Oaks Dr., Raleigh, NC, 27614

ISBN 978-1-941103-46-3
Copyright © 2014 by Trina Bresser Matous
Cover design by writelydesigned.com
Interior design by Karthick Srinivasan

Scripture taken from the New King James Version®. Copyright © 1982 by Thomas Nelson. Used by permission. All rights reserved.

Available in print from your local bookstore, online, or from the publisher at: www.lighthousepublishingofthecarolinas.com

Follow the author online at: @TBresserMatous or facebook.com/TBresserMatous

All rights reserved. Non-commercial interests may reproduce portions of this book without the express written permission of Lighthouse Publishing of the Carolinas, provided the text does not exceed 500 words. When reproducing text from this book, include the following credit line: "The Epistles of James, Peter, and Jude by Trina Bresser Matous published by Lighthouse Publishing of the Carolinas. Used by permission."

Brought to you by the creative team at
LighthousePublishingoftheCarolinas.com:
Eddie Jones, Barbara King, Brian Cross, and Meaghan Burnett.

Library of Congress Cataloging-in-Publication Data
Bresser Matous, Trina
The Epistles of James, Peter, and Jude / Trina Bresser Matous 1st ed.

Printed in the United States of America

Praise for *The Epistles Of James, Peter, And Jude*

As a Bible study leader of eighteen years, I found *The Epistles of James, Peter, and Jude: Christian Living Bible Study Series* by Trina Bresser Matous to be a very succinct study plan for reading through these powerful New Testament books. Trina offers a brief, but thorough Introduction to how to study the Bible, then examines each chapter with Background, Overview, and Insights sections.

Trina has provided a powerful tool to enable either individuals or groups to move through these epistles in a simple and perceptive manner. The writing is excellent and the spiritual insights are powerful. This book is a valuable Bile study tool for Bible students.

Norma Gail
Bible Study Leader, Speaker
Author of, *Land of My Dreams*

Unlike many Bible studies, Trina Bresser Matous breaks down *The Epistles of James, Peter, and Jude* into understandable and clear truths. Trina uses godly insight to give the reader background information along with overview and insight at the end of each chapter. What a great way to understand timeless Biblical teachings.

Jane Jenkins Herlong, CSP
Speaker and author of *Bury Me With My Pearls*

Trina Bresser Matous is a gifted tour guide, walking the reader through the complexities and context of scripture. If you're looking for a deeper understanding of *The Epistles of James, Peter, and Jude,* Trina is your gal. Don't miss it!

Allison Allen
Speaker and author

When we challenged our congregation with an ambitious Bible reading plan (The Life Journal), Trina was asked to write a refresher commentary to help guide those looking to more accurately understand the Biblical text as they read. Her work exceeded our expectations. Trina's thoughtful insights into both the Old and New Testament ministered to hundreds of our members every week as the reading plan unfolded. Our congregants snapped her study material off our church shelves every week. I am thrilled that this same resource is now available to a wider audience. Readers will be blessed!

Bryan Hochhalter
Lead Pastor, Grace Community Church (March, 2014)

In a world where so many feel that truth is up for grabs, knowing God's word and its background is critical in helping us live lives that reflect His glory. Trina Bresser Matous does a phenomenal job of researching the background of the Bible and pulling out insights that are applicable to life. This volume would be a blessing for any who want to not only know the Bible, but know how to apply the Bible to his or her life.

Wayne Stapleton
Pastor, Renewal Church

Nearly a decade ago our church launched a comprehensive effort to encourage Bible reading in our congregation. In an effort to bring the readings to life, promote discussion and application within the body, Trina Bresser Matous invested full time efforts reading ahead and creating overview notes of the upcoming weeks' readings. Her thorough research, summary and application notes were a huge catalyst to our body's daily engagement with the Scriptures. Over a number of years her work was updated and perfected. We are thrilled that this tool has now become bound in an easy to use series that can now be enjoyed by the larger body of Christ. You will find using these supplements, in conjunction with your own Bible reading and study, an enormous encouragement.

Bryce Gray
Elder, Grace Community Church

Get wisdom and with all your getting, get understanding.
Proverbs 4.7

The depth to which Trina poured her heart into conveying clarity and understanding was only matched by the accuracy of the details given. As an active participant within a church-wide Bible study, I found this resource to be comprehensive, honest and a passionate harvesting of the WORD of God.

Trina's account and interpretation of each book is more than background research, and more than fragmented expositions culled from other commentators. It is a compelling, Spirit led study guide and companion tool. If you are in search of an easy to follow, well outlined approach to studying that remains faithful to the truth of God's Word, look no further!

Dr. Zora Smith Denson
Educational Consultant

Dedication

To my parents, Jean and Jerry

What a blessing that my siblings and I are committed believers, in large part because our parents taught us about the faith and modeled Christian life every day.

Introduction

The Epistles of James, Peter, and Jude is designed to assist you in your relationship with God by helping you understand difficult passages, better appreciating statements made within the confines of ancient cultural practices, and shedding new light on familiar verses. As you learn more about the history and purpose of each verse, you will find yourself growing in wisdom and knowledge.

The four epistles written by James, Peter, and Jude serve as a practical set of instructions on how to live the Christian life. Though none of these men were particularly doctrinal in their writings, they covered many practical applications for living in a manner that reflects the teachings and life of Jesus.

Each man encouraged his readers to diligently pursue the characteristics that transformed them more and more into the image of Christ. By doing so, believers in the twenty-first century will learn, among other things, why genuine faith reveals itself in action, how to live in the midst of unjust suffering, how all believers (not just wives to their husbands) are called to submit, and how knowledge of the truth will protect against false teachings.

Reading the Bible can be a daunting task. Verses often require a great deal of study, prayer and meditation in order to gain an adequate understanding. But don't loose heart! God reveals His Word to those who earnestly seek Him (Jer. 29:13). This chapter-by-chapter series will help you discover the riches of the Bible.

How to use this book

The information given on the following pages should be read in conjunction with the Biblical text. I recommend you read the Biblical text first, then read the associated comments. As you do, ask the Holy Spirit for wisdom and insight.

I have attempted to make the information presented here non-translation specific. You may find, however, that a particular word being discussed does not appear in the translation you are using. The concept still applies. If you want to find the specific word being discussed, try looking at different translations, which are easily accessible online.

God's Word has many purposes. He uses it to communicate His great love for and mercy toward all of humanity. He also uses it to speak into our lives. For unbelievers, God uses His Word to draw them into faith. For newer believers, He might use it to inform and grow their faith. For all believers, God uses His Word to mold and shape us more and more into the image of His Son. James reminded his readers that simply hearing God's Word was not enough; they needed to do it as well (Jam.

1.22). Questions at the end of each chapter are intended to be a catalyst to applying the Biblical text to our lives and experiences in the 21st century. I encourage you to seek and be open to the leading of the Holy Spirit. Spend time thinking about your responses while being sensitive to promptings of the Holy Spirit to change attitudes, behaviors, or thought patterns.

Use in a small group setting

God uses other believers as well as His Word in our lives. Discussing the chapter-end questions in a small group setting can be beneficial. Other believers' viewpoints and insights can enhance our own understanding of the Biblical text in ways we may not gain on our own. They can also aid our understanding of and response to the trials, hardships, and difficulties we face in our lives. God tells us that we "sharpen" each other as we relate together over His word and what He is doing in our lives. (Prov. 27:17)

God's Word is called the Living Word because God continually reveals new insights. Your insights from a passage may be different than a friend's. This is okay!

Don't be discouraged if your knowledge of the Bible and understanding of the text does not seem as comprehensive as someone else's. God is pleased with anyone who opens His Word and will reveal Himself through it.

Do be encouraged that as you continue to read, pieces will fit together, new understandings will surface, and revelations will emerge.

Remember that God is gracious and merciful. He wants a relationship with you through His Son, Jesus Christ. So take a breath, enjoy His Word, and come to know Him better.

Enjoy your journey with God. His Word is rich and will add meaning to your life!

Table Of Contents

Praise for The Epistles Of James, Peter, And Jude iii
Dedication vii
Introduction viii
Table Of Contents xii

JAMES

James 1 3
James 2 8
James 3 12
James 4 16
James 5 20

FIRST PETER

1 Peter 1 25
1 Peter 2 29
1 Peter 3 33
1 Peter 4 37
1 Peter 5 41

SECOND PETER

2 Peter 1 46
2 Peter 2 50
2 Peter 3 54

JUDE

Jude 59

Acknowledgements 63

JAMES

The book of James is a how-to manual filled with instructions for living the Christian life. In this sense, it is one of the most practical books of the New Testament. James wrote his letter to address not only the problems many believers were facing but to point out the dangers that could result from not addressing the problems. Understanding the Christian faith and putting it into practical use could avoid such dangers.

Though James is much more practical than doctrinal, the major theological issue in the book is faith vs. works. Some have tried to argue that this means salvation is earned through works, but it is clear from James' writing that he was addressing people already practicing saving faith. James was focusing on the natural result of faith. Faith that is alive and growing in Christ will show itself by engaging in the work of Christ.

The writer of James is not known with certainty, though it is clearly named after its author. The New Testament mentions four men named James: the son of Zebedee and brother of John (Matt. 10.2), the son of Alphaeus (Lk. 6.15), the father of Judas (not Iscariot; Luke 6.16), and the half brother of Jesus (Matt. 13.55; Gal. 1.19). Almost nothing is known of either the son of Alphaeus or the father of Judas, making it unlikely either of these men wrote the letter. James, the son of Zebedee, was part of Jesus' inner circle along with Peter and John. He could potentially have written the letter, though he was martyred in 44 AD, a date considered too early for the letter to have been written. The final candidate, Jesus' half brother, is considered the most likely and traditionally held to be the author.

The twelve tribes scattered abroad (Jam. 1.1) likely means James wrote to Jewish Christians outside of Palestine with the intent that the letter would be passed among multiple churches. Because the letter contains no references to the Jerusalem council of AD 49 (over which James presided), the conflict between Jew and Gentile that developed in the church as it grew, or the melding of Jews and Gentiles into one body of believers, it is thought the letter was written fairly early, sometime between AD 45 and 49.

The book can be divided into three parts. The first, 1.1-18, focuses on the tests of faith. The second, 1.19-5.6, addresses the characteristics of faith, while the final part, 5.7-20, deals with the triumph of faith.

JAMES 1

BACKGROUND

God tested Abraham when He asked Abraham to sacrifice his son, Isaac. The test proved Abraham's loyalty to God and resulted in blessings upon Abraham (Gen. 22.1-18).

Several Biblical passages refer to the rewards believers will one day enjoy (Matt. 5.12; Luke. 6.35; Col. 3.24). Such rewards include garments (Rev. 3.5; 19.7-8) and crowns (1 Cor. 9.25; Rev. 2.10).

Mirrors in ancient times were fairly rare and did not produce the clear images of today's mirrors. As a result, people rarely saw what they looked like.

OVERVIEW

Though trials often resulted in hardship, James stated there were reasons to be joyful in the midst of them.

Faith being tested has a sense of being refined rather than seeing whether one would pass a test or not. Refining is a part of maturing and is an essential part of every believer's faith journey.

Trials produce the maturity necessary to remain *faithful* (*persevere*) over a lifetime. The end result is believers who are wise, well-grounded, and complete in their faith.

Wisdom is not the same as information. God gives a new perspective, appreciation, or ability to discern in the midst of trials. He does not necessarily provide the answers or way to get out of the trial.

James' admonition not to doubt does not refer to the moments of uncertainty all believers experience from time to time. Instead, he is talking about a divided allegiance or loyalty that results in being partially set on God and partially set on the world.

The *humble* (*lowly*) likely refers to the poor, in contrast to the rich. The rich should not put too much stock in their wealth because it is unlikely to last.

Enduring trials are one way of demonstrating love for Christ and will be rewarded with a crown of life.

James listed five stages of temptation: *curiosity* (*desire*), *enticement* (*conceived*), *conception* (*birth*), *maturity* (*full-grown*), and *termination* (*death*). Sin that matures and is full-grown has become a lifestyle.

God's testing is always designed to mature believers in their faith. He does not tempt them in hopes they will fail. As a result, God should not be blamed for leading one to sin. The choice is always the individual's. As further proof that God does not tempt, James reminded his readers that God is responsible for *all* that is good.

Giving birth through the *word of truth* may refer to humanity's initial creation through God's spoken word or to rebirth through faith in the gospel. In either case, God giving birth is contrasted with desire giving birth.

One means of combating temptation is to listen before speaking and guard against becoming angry. Unrighteous anger does not display God's grace in a person's life but rather points toward sin and vindication. Since both God the Father and God the Son displayed anger, anger in and of itself is not sinful. It becomes sinful when believers respond with ungodliness, malice, rage, and revenge.

Hearing the word of God was (is) not enough. Believers had to be obedient to it, as well.

James said the law brought *freedom* (*liberty*) because God designed the law to free us from sin and protect us from much of the evil in the world.

James admonished his readers to practice a pure religion that did not consist of superficial ritual but showed care and concern for the most helpless and unprotected in society.

INSIGHTS

Finding joy in the midst of trial does not negate the pain and suffering we may experience as a result of the trial. James was not suggesting that believers put on a happy face and pretend the pain and suffering do not exist. Rather, joy results from a long-term perspective. We can experience a deep sense of joy because we know that God is in control of all that happens, that He is at work in us to mature us in our faith, and through us to bring His Word and saving grace to those around us. God has promised to use all things, including our trials, to bring about good for those who believe (us!) in Him (Rom. 8.28). That is worth being joyful about!

1. James encouraged his readers to count their trials among their joys because of the perseverance and patience that comes when their faith is tested. Do you have this perspective when you face any kind of trial? Why do you think James could have such a positive outlook when facing hardship and suffering? What can you do to find greater joy in your hardships, sufferings, and trials?

2. Can you claim to follow James' advice to be quick to listen, slow to speak, and slow to anger? Why is it so tempting to jump in and speak without fully listening to whoever is speaking? What are some of the benefits to giving others the opportunity to express themselves without interruption? Why does James mention anger along with listening and speaking? If you are in the habit of getting angry quickly, how can you bring your temper under control and be more honoring in your responses?

JAMES 2

BACKGROUND

In Roman society, civil law favored the upper classes. Those in a lower class could not bring suit against those in a higher class. Penalties for the same offense were often more severe for those in a lower class than those in a higher class.

OVERVIEW

Class divisions were well defined in the first century. The new Christian faith, however, was open to all people and promoted equality before God. James admonished his readers not to practice the partiality or favoritism that was prevalent in their world. He included four reasons for this: God Himself embraced the poor (v. 5), it was often the rich initiating persecution against Christians (vv. 6-7), Christ's command to love one's neighbors had no restricting stipulations (vv. 8-11), and judgment will come on those who violate God's commands (vv. 12-13).

Unlike much of the world at large, God does not determine a person's value based on what they have or do not have. Instead, His test is based on a person's love of and obedience to Him. As a result, many who are marginalized by the world are valued in God's kingdom. Inheriting God's kingdom includes reigning with Christ.

The *royal* law is the law of love. It trumps all other laws. Observing some parts of the law and rejecting other parts still results in breaking the law. All sin is equal in God's eyes, so transgressing the law in a small way (such as showing partiality) is no better than transgressing it in a major way (such as committing adultery or murder).

Believers will be judged in the same manner in which they judge others. If they show mercy, they will receive mercy. But if they fail to show mercy, they will not experience mercy themselves.

James used an example to show that faith well-placed and alive in God would naturally show itself in mercy toward and good works for others. Believers experience God's love and mercy because of the work He does in their lives. In a similar manner, as image bearers of God, those who have faith in Him will show it in the care and concern they have for those around them.

Verses 18-19, introduced by *someone will say*, are the words of an objector. The gist of the objector's statements is that there is no relationship between faith and works. In response, James offered two examples to show that genuine faith naturally showed itself in works. Abraham was counted as righteous as a result of his obedient willingness to sacrifice his son. The act was evidence of his faith. James used *justified* to mean *proved*, i.e., Abraham proved his faith by what he did. In a similar manner, Rahab's faith would not have been evident to anyone had she not demonstrated it by offering lodging to the spies. The relationship between faith and works was just as crucial as the spirit is to the body.

INSIGHTS

James' reminder to avoid favoritism is just as valid today as it was in the first century. It is a human tendency to judge people by their looks or the amount of money they have. Many people have been turned away from church and thereby faith in Christ because they did not meet the perception the church membership had as to how attendees dress or the amount of money they make. Favoritism within the body of believers is not to be tolerated. In His eyes, there are no divisions; rich and poor, educated and uneducated, beautiful and plain. All are called into His kingdom– on earth and in heaven.

1. James warned against showing favoritism. What are some subtle or not so subtle ways favoritism can creep into our daily practices, thoughts, and behaviors? What role does judgment play in showing favoritism? Does knowing a person's story encourage or discourage showing favoritism? How can you guard against showing favoritism in your encounters with other people?

2. What is the relationship between faith and works James articulates? Why would he state that faith without works is dead? What role do works or good deeds play in your faith? Is there a place for you to express more of your faith through good deeds?

James 3

BACKGROUND

James was not the only one to warn those who had influence over other people's understanding of the truth. Jesus repeatedly came into conflict with the Pharisees because their interpretation of the law contradicted God's intent for it. Jesus not only warned the people to beware of the example and influence the Pharisees set (Matt. 16.6) but warned the Pharisees themselves that the influence they wielded on those around them would not go without judgment (Matt. 23.13-29).

OVERVIEW

James' warning about teaching was not an exhortation not to teach but to be fully aware of the greater judgment teachers would face because of the influence they have in leading people. The warning applied not only to those who would pursue teaching but to James as well.

James used speaking as the litmus test for whether one had reached perfection or not, rightly stating that no one had. Though the tongue appears small and insignificant, it holds great influence over one's ability to be sinless. He used three examples to make his point. The first two illustrate seemingly small and insignificant tools that actually have the greatest ability to direct that on which they were used. The third example demonstrates the extensively damaging impact the tongue can have. James' use of *hell* suggests that Satan is behind some of what is spoken through the ideas he puts in people's heads (Mk. 8.33; Acts 5.3).

Though animals can be trained to respond as desired, completely controlling the tongue is beyond a person's ability.

James pointed out the inconsistency of praising God in one breath and cursing people (made in the image of God) in the next. James again followed his statement with examples. James used the examples to make it clear that the believers' nature was apparent by their words. Those who cursed others made in the image of God were using their praises to cover over their true nature.

Success in controlling the tongue comes primarily from working on one's inner self. James stated the solution to an uncontrolled tongue is divine wisdom (*wisdom from above*). Evidence of such wisdom is shown in the deeds one does with humility. Worldly wisdom, which is little more than self-interest, has no value and great ability to corrupt. Relying on such wisdom causes confusion, allows evil to gain a foothold, and results in havoc.

In contrast, divine wisdom has nothing about it that is self-serving. It naturally reflects God's purity or freedom from defilement. *Peace-loving (peaceable)* does not suggest compromising the truth simply to keep the peace. Rather, it indicates a tranquility and calmness. The outcome of such an attitude is not just greater peace but righteousness as well.

INSIGHTS

James' warning about the tongue should be heeded today. Each of us has the ability to do great good or great harm simply by what we say. Often we attempt to dismiss hurtful statements by qualifying them with, "I was only kidding (joking)." Yet, they can still be very hurtful. It is much better to leave such things unsaid than to say them and leave a lingering hurt, whether you meant it or not. On the other hand, we often miss opportunities to encourage and bless another person because we leave unsaid what deserves to be spoken. A good rule of thumb is to say to others what we ourselves would want to hear.

1. Why does James put such emphasis on the tongue? Why does James suggest an animal can be tamed but the tongue cannot? What is the relationship between what you say and what you do? What can you do to better praise God and honor those around you with your tongue?

2. Why does James distinguish between heavenly and earthly wisdom? How can you go about obtaining heavenly wisdom?

JAMES 4

BACKGROUND

Diatribe was an ancient literary teaching technique in which the writer used rhetorical questions, rhetorical exaggeration, hyperbole, and imaginary opponents. James used the technique several times throughout his letter, including when he stated that his readers were murderers (4.2). In all likelihood, they were not, though he made the statement to emphasize his point.

OVERVIEW

The inward battle of desires for pleasure versus desires to do God's will has the outward effect of causing conflict and strife among believers. Desires for pleasure most often are evidenced in material things and can reveal themselves through coveting and envy.

James answered an unspoken objection by stating that the readers were not experiencing answers to prayer because they were praying with selfish motives instead of motives to do God's will.

James used adultery in a figurative sense to illustrate

misplaced loyalty believers have when they begin following the ways of the world instead of God's ways. Such loyalty is not displayed in occasional sin but in habitual sin that becomes a lifestyle.

It is unclear whether the *spirit who dwells in us* is the Holy Spirit reflecting God's jealousy when His people leave Him for the world or the human spirit with a covetous desire. In either case, James' quote of Prov. 3.34 makes it clear that those who oppose God will face a formidable foe while those who seek God will enjoy His grace.

James offered two pieces of advice to his readers to avoid becoming *friends* with the world. First, yield to God by obediently seeking and doing His will. Second, oppose and fight against temptation. When Satan sees believers strengthened by the Holy Spirit, he has no other option but to flee.

God is always ready to respond to those who seek after Him and take steps toward Him. Drawing near to the holy God may require repentance on the part of the believer. Signs of repentance include: purifying one's heart, grieving and mourning, and humbling oneself before God. The outcome of such effort is often being exalted in ways the believer could never achieve on his/her own.

James returned one last time to his theme of not passing judgment on others. Judging others was contrary to the law and placed one outside the law in judgment of it. Only one person is qualified to judge the law and that is God.

James did not suggest that making plans is wrong. Instead, doing so without consulting God or realizing how quickly life can change and even end is prideful and evil.

INSIGHTS

Although planning for the future is prudent, such plans must be held loosely. In reality, we have no idea what the future holds. We all know of someone who was killed suddenly in an accident, died unexpectedly from a fatal disease, or wasted away from a terminal illness. Only God's grace prevents the same from happening to us. When we take on financial debt, or put off until tomorrow what *should* be done today, we presume upon a future that is not in any way guaranteed to us. As we make our plans, we are best off living as fully as we can in the only day we have, today, and thanking God for the gift of each new day He gives us.

1. Have you ever considered what causes the fights and quarrels you get into? Are they motivated by a godly desire to serve others or a selfish desire to get what you want? James states that his readers were not getting from God what they wanted because they were asking with the wrong motive. What is the right motive? How can you change your motives to be more in line with God's? What happens to your requests when your motives are godly in nature?

2. Does James suggest that we should not make any plans for the future? How can we ensure that our plans for the future fall within the Lord's will?

JAMES 5

BACKGROUND

James' denunciations of the rich were timely. Approximately thirty years after James wrote his letter, almost the entire Jewish aristocracy was wiped out in the Jewish revolt against Rome.

Anointing oil was used in the Old Testament to consecrate people, kings, and others to God. In ancient times, oil was thought to have medicinal properties. It was often used to cleanse wounds or to anoint someone who wanted to be protected against disease.

OVERVIEW

As James continued to exhort his readers, he was not condemning the rich out of hand but condemning some of the practices that often accompanied being rich. The three main evidences of wealth were abundant food, expensive clothing, and precious metals. James expressed how unreliable they were for maintaining lasting wealth by pointing to their temporary nature and their eventual destruction.

Mosaic Law prohibited withholding a worker's wages, even overnight (Deut. 24.14-15; Lev. 19.13). Gaining wealth through this means was (is!) fraudulent and deceitful.

Scholars have interpreted *you have fattened yourselves in the day of slaughter* in two ways. It could mean over-indulgence during feasts and celebrations. It could also be more eschatological (end times) in nature by referring to people's self-fattening of their soul for their own slaughter.

Having addressed the risks associated with being rich, James turned to the oppressed as he encouraged them to be patient when injustice occurred. The Lord's return would right all that had been wronged. James used three examples to encourage patience. First was the farmer who could only wait for the seed to produce its crop. Second were the prophets who patiently endured suffering as they spoke God's word to the people. Third was Job, who suffered for reasons unknown to him but patiently lived through the circumstances in which he found himself.

James' warning against swearing was related to taking an oath. In ancient times, as today, people often invoked different objects to confirm the validity of their statement. Such statements risked breaking the commandment to keep holy God's name or placed the speaker in a position of breaking his/her oath when what was stated did not come to pass.

Anointing a sick person with oil may have represented a combination of using the medicinal properties of oil along with handing the illness over to God. The passage makes clear, however, that it is prayer that brings healing. Sickness is *sometimes* the result of sin (Matt. 9.2; Jn 9.1-3). In such cases, confession of sin becomes a prerequisite for healing.

James pointed to Elijah as an example of an ordinary person whose fervent prayer was answered (1 Kings 17-18).

One of the most significant things one person can do for another is to save his/her life. Sharing God's word with an unbeliever can have the same effect. Eternal death is just as permanent as physical death, and the opportunity to save one from such a sentence should be seized.

INSIGHTS

Though humans have a tendency to blame God for their suffering, James' statement that God extends compassion and mercy is worth remembering. As in the case of Job, God permits suffering in order that His purposes may be met. Additionally, we may think our suffering is God's fault when in reality it is the result of selfishness and corruption on either or both our part or the part of other human beings. God is just, compassionate, and merciful. He is constantly at work in the lives of those who believe in Him. Though suffering is difficult, only

God can use it to bring about unimaginable results for our good and blessing.

1. James admonished his readers not to swear. Why would he make such a statement? Why is swearing displeasing to God? What role, if any, does swearing play in your life? What can you do to minimize your use of swearing? What words does God want you to use in place of swearing?

2. James stressed the role prayer and praise should play in his readers' lives. Do prayer and praise play such a role in your life? How quickly do you turn to your fellow believers to hold you up in prayer during times of need? Do you seek forgiveness from those you have sinned against? Do you seek to remain righteous before God so that you prayers will be powerful and effective?

FIRST PETER

Peter is believed to have written his first epistle in approximately 63 AD, before Nero's great persecution of the Jews started, yet after widespread persecution had already begun to take place. The epistle addresses the believer's response in the face of persecution and suffering. Such a response must be prefaced by an attitude of submission as modeled by Christ: citizens are to submit to the government, laborers to their overseers, wives to husbands, husbands to wives, and Christians to each other.

Once Peter had fully explained submission, he moved to the area of suffering. Though suffering can be difficult to live through, especially when it is the result of persecution, joyful acceptance and appreciation for God's work in the midst of it leads to the ultimate submission to the hand of God in one's life.

Peter's introduction (*pilgrims of the Dispersion*, 1.1) and warning about behavior (*honorable among the Gentiles*, 2.12) would, at first glance, indicate the letter had been written to Jewish Christians. However, other statements (*called out of darkness*, 2.9; *once not a people but now the people of God*, 2.10) indicate Peter's audience was primarily Gentile believers.

First Peter can be divided into three parts. The first, 1.1-2.12, focuses on the hope of salvation. The second, 2.13-3.12, addresses submission of believers. The final part, 3.13-5.14, discusses believers' suffering in light of Christ's suffering.

1 Peter 1

BACKGROUND

Pontus, Galatia, Cappadocia, Asia, and Bithynia were all provinces in what is today primarily Turkey. While it is apparent that, by the time of Peter's writing, there were Christians in each of these provinces, the history of how this occurred is only partially known. Paul passed through Galatia on all three of his missionary journeys and Asia on his last two. Pilgrims from Pontus, Cappadocia, and Asia were present at the Pentecost (Acts 2.9). How churches were established in Bithynia is unknown.

OVERVIEW

Believers' salvation comes solely through the mercy of God. Each was physically born a first time, and then experienced a second, spiritual birth when they placed their faith in the death and resurrection of Christ. The result of such faith is an inheritance that can never be perverted, spoiled, or diminished.

Salvation is great reason to rejoice. Before its ultimate

realization, however, various trials (i.e., no one type of problem) will cause suffering that will be used by God to mature one in his/her faith.

Relatively few people had the privilege of seeing Jesus, yet all those who place their faith in Him can experience the unspeakable joy that results from the security of salvation.

The prophets were not trying to find out *if* salvation would occur but *when*: when Christ would come and when the end of the age would occur.

The prophets did not make up the message on a whim or out of their own imagination. The Spirit of Christ was responsible for the message the prophets spoke.

God revealed to the prophets that the message they preached would not come to pass in their lifetimes but to a later generation.

Girding up one's loins meant to gather one's long robes and tuck them into their belt to make running or moving about easier. In a similar manner, Peter encouraged his readers to prepare themselves for action, to focus on those things that needed their attention while not being distracted by trivial things.

Obedience was a highly valued trait in children by both the Jewish and Roman cultures. Peter called his readers to be obedient as children to their faith and God's calling on their lives. In this manner, believers would put behind them their old sinful ways and seek to model their behavior on the holiness of God.

Though believers embrace God as Father, they are not exempt from the coming judgment. All people will be judged. Believers will enjoy eternal life with God, yet will still experience God's judgment regarding what they did while on earth.

Redeem carries a sense of regaining or freeing something by some means of payment. Believers were redeemed from their bondage to the world through the sacrificial blood of Christ.

The means of salvation was known to God before the beginning of time and was revealed to all who would hear through the life, death, and resurrection of Christ.

Believers are able to purify their souls by being obedient to God's Word. Purifying themselves leads to loving others in obedience to and as a reflection of God. Peter quoted Isaiah 40.6-8 from the Septuagint (the Greek translation of the Hebrew Scriptures) to emphasize the incorruptible nature into which believers have been reborn.

INSIGHTS

Gold is viewed as one of the most prized and costly items in the world. Yet Peter says that faith in God is far more precious and longer lasting than the purest gold. We often don't view our faith as precious and worthy of valuing greatly. Yet in the broad scheme of life and eternity, our faith in Christ gives us far more than *anything* on earth we might choose to value. Our faith not only results in a fuller, more fulfilled, and more joyful life on earth, we also will enjoy the privilege of spending eternity with God.

1. Why does Peter call hope in God the Father a living hope? Why is this hope different from the hope we can put in anything else? Why does this hope lead to an inheritance that cannot be spoiled in any way?

2. Peter reminded his readers that they were called to be holy because God is holy. How do you strive to live a holy life? What tempts you away from living the life God is calling you to? Is there anything you need to confess and repent to God? What are the next steps you need to take to live the holy life God desires?

1 Peter 2

BACKGROUND

In ancient times, placement of the cornerstone on the foundation was critical. The remainder of the building was built out and up from this cornerstone. If it was not laid accurately, the whole of the building would be affected.

In Greek, the word *governor* was used for any person who held a position of authority on behalf of the government.

OVERVIEW

The five terms Peter listed, *malice*, *deceit*, *hypocrisy*, *envy*, and *evil speaking*, all have at their base an ill feeling toward or a desire for ill to come to another.

Peter used the analogy of a newborn's need for milk to indicate the strong longing with which believers should seek the Word of God. Just as mother's milk is necessary for the growth and health of the newborn, so God's Word will bring maturity and spiritual health to the believer.

The old temple was made of stone while the new temple is built from the living stone of believers, thereby creating the church. In this building Christ serves as the chief cornerstone.

In the Old Testament, only male members of the tribe of Levi were eligible to become priests. In the new temple, all believers are priests with the responsibility of serving God.

Peter quoted Is. 26.16, Ps. 118.22, and Is. 8.14, which are all linked by their reference to stone. The first speaks of the peace believers will have in placing their trust in the Cornerstone on which their faith is built. The second two speak of the unbeliever's rejection of this same Cornerstone. Unbelievers stumble on the Cornerstone because of their refusal to trust in Christ.

In contrast to those who don't believe, believers are part of God's chosen people. One of the purposes of being part of God's family is to declare to the rest of the world the marvelous works God has done.

Peter's use of *sojourners* and *pilgrims* was a reminder that believers are travelers on their way to their home—heaven. Many of the trials and sufferings experienced in this life are a result of being in a place other than the one intended for believers. In spite of their trials, believers are to maintain a good testimony to God so that the good works believers do might draw unbelievers into belief.

Peter states that submission to the governing

authorities is an expectation held of all believers; it is not the result of individual choice. It was not Peter who was commanding submission but God. God desired that those who believed in Him would do good and thereby draw others to place their trust in God as well.

False teachers tried to rationalize forgiveness of sins that resulted from faith in Christ as a freedom to do anything one desired. Peter called this rationalization a *cloak for vice* and stated that believers are to serve God rather than look for justification for filling their own personal desires.

Peter called on all in positions of servanthood to be obedient to those over them, especially when they are unjustly punished. This would give a good testimony to God. This admonition can also be applied to employees and employers.

Jesus was the ultimate example of silently suffering in the face of unjust persecution. His suffering allows all believers to receive spiritual health.

INSIGHTS

Today, rationalizations abound for not following all the rules and laws the government sets for its citizens. These include, for instance, not paying all the tax one should, not registering for military service, and defrauding social services. Yet Peter's reminder that believers are commanded to be obedient to the governing authorities is just as relevant today as it was then. The only time we are free to disobey a law is when it is in direct violation of God's law (such as abortion or the redefinition of marriage to extend beyond one man and one woman). God will use our obedience to laws we do not agree with to bring glory to Himself.

1. Peter reminded his readers that they should submit to the authority God has placed over them. Do you submit to the authorities placed over you? Do you pray regularly that those who lead you at work, spiritually, in your city, state, and/or country are hearing from God, punishing those who do wrong, and commending those who do right?

2. What does it mean to be God's chosen generation, royal priesthood, and holy nation? Does God have expectations for those He calls to be His special people? How does knowing you are royal and holy affect the way you live?

1 Peter 3

BACKGROUND

Well-to-do women in Peter's day often adorned their hair in elaborate styles. This and other fashions could be quite expensive to maintain and were designed to draw attention to themselves.

OVERVIEW

Just as citizens are to submit to the authority of the government and slaves to their masters, so wives are to submit to the authority of their husbands. All wives, but especially those with unbelieving husbands, were not to preach to their husbands but to encourage them and win them over with their loving acts.

Chaste conduct meant righteousness or lack of moral fault. Such conduct was to be accompanied by *fear*, meaning respect for God.

Peter was not condemning women who styled their hair, wore jewelry, or dressed in fine clothes. Instead, he was encouraging women to pay attention to their inward appearance (*character*) as much as they did to their outward appearance. The things that adorned the outward appearance would one day fade away but those things that developed the character would remain.

Sarah's use of *lord* in reference to her husband was a sign of respect. It is akin to the use of *sir* today.

Husbands are to be aware of their wives' needs, dreams, and desires in order that they may respond to them in the best way possible.

Weaker vessel refers primarily to physical weakness.

Since God designed marriage to reflect the relationship within the Godhead, a husband who does not treat his wife well is likely to experience a lack of answers to prayer.

Peter concluded his instruction on submitting by encouraging believers to put the needs of others first. Compassion suggests a willingness to have the same feelings as, or suffer with, another person.

Believers are to respond to evil with blessings. Returning evil for evil is called vengeance, a position God clearly reserves for Himself alone (Lev. 19.18; Deut. 32.35). Peter quoted Ps. 34.12-16 to support his point.

Generally, those who do good are less likely to be harmed by others than those who do evil. When suffering does occur, believers should ensure it is the result of serving God rather than discipline for sin.

False teachings about Christianity were rampant in Peter's time (just as they are today). Peter encouraged his readers to know their faith well enough that they could speak its truth whenever necessary.

Eventually, those who falsely accuse Christians will one day realize the error of their ways.

The suffering believers experience does not equal, but does bring to mind, the suffering of Christ and His saving death and resurrection. The meaning of *spirits in prison* is not clear. Some believe it means Jesus preached in the place where the fallen angels are held captive. Others believe it refers to human spirits and means that Christ preached through Noah to those in his time who rejected God.

Peter does not say that water baptism provides salvation but that it is a symbolic act done by those who have trusted in the life, death, and resurrection of Christ.

INSIGHTS

Peter's admonition against paying too much attention to outward appearances is just as valid today as it was in his time. The world places tremendous emphasis for males as well as females on appearance. Anti-aging products and a myriad of treatments are designed to remove blemishes to one's appearance. In their place, such treatments may not be bad, but the continual emphasis on their importance conceals the greater importance of developing one's character. Strong character will always outlast good looks. In addition, strong character will be of much greater value over the course of a lifetime than perfect looks.

1. Both wives and husbands are called to honor their spouses in specific ways. If you are married, is this difficult for you? Does knowing you are honoring God and Jesus make it any easier? If you are not married and one day hope to be, have you thought about how you would honor your spouse as Peter suggests? Are there any attitudes or behaviors you would have to change in order to do so?

2. Are you prepared to give an answer for the hope that lies within you, as Peter suggests you should be? Can you articulate why believing and putting your faith and hope in Christ is better than anything the world can offer? Do those around you know you are a believer just from observing your behavior and actions?

1 Peter 4

BACKGROUND

Hospitality was highly valued in ancient times. Extending hospitality to strangers could mean housing and feeding them for two to three days with no expectation of payment.

Peter expounded very briefly on spiritual gifts in 4.10-11. Other passages that give greater detail include Rom. 12.3-8, 1 Cor. 12-14, and Eph. 4.1-16.

OVERVIEW

Christ's suffering *in the flesh* means that His suffering was just as real as any suffering all other humans experience. Fully living the Christian life means being prepared to suffer for the truth of Christ. The focus of such a life is on fulfilling the will of God rather than following the sinful passions of the flesh.

Unbelievers cannot understand the transformation that occurs in the lives of believers as they leave their former behaviors behind and embrace lifestyles that are pleasing to God. Unbelievers think they can live in any manner in which they choose but fail to realize they will one day stand in judgment before God.

There are several interpretations for the meaning of the gospel being preached to the *dead*. The most likely is that Peter was referring to those who once were spiritually dead. Their faith in Christ leads to man's judgment that often results in persecution but allows them to live according to the ways of God.

Peter encouraged his readers to pray diligently and be watchful in the times of suffering that would accompany the end times.

The Christian life is most effectively demonstrated through the love Christians have among themselves and, by extension, to those around them.

A believer's love covering the sin of an unbeliever does not mean the unbeliever will not be judged for his/her sins. Rather, love covers sin because it does not tempt others to sin. It readily forgives those who have sinned and does not talk about the past sins of another.

Peter clearly states that every believer has been gifted in some manner to serve God and the body of believers. God did not give believers their gifts for their own personal use or pleasure but to fulfill His will. In this way, they are stewards of what He has graciously given. Peter listed two gifts. *Speaking* likely refers to the gift of prophecy, while *ministering* means serving. Whatever their gift, believers are to rely on God as the source of their power to accomplish His will.

As Peter returned again to the issue of suffering, he encouraged believers to expect suffering rather than think it unlikely to occur. They were to rejoice when suffering, especially suffering unjustly, because they would be blessed and experience reward in the next life. Peter warned, however, that suffering experienced as punishment for sin would not bring blessing. Only the suffering experienced on behalf of Christ would bring blessing. Such suffering should not be experienced with shame but with full glory and praise to God.

Judgment does not always mean that condemnation will follow. Believers will experience a judgment that will evaluate their works on earth. *Those who do not obey* are unbelievers who will suffer the judgment of condemnation. *Scarcely saved* refers to the mercy of God that allows people to experience salvation at all.

INSIGHTS

Some of the false teachings Peter and the other first-century writers wrote against are still prevalent today. In the name of Christianity, some teach that suffering results from an inadequate relationship with God, while a lack of material items (Cadillac, 10,000 square foot home, big bank account, etc.) or illness results when a believer does not have *enough* faith. When evaluated against God's Word as found in the Bible, these and other similar teachings are clearly false. The Biblical writers *promise* there will be suffering. God does not promise material riches or healing, but does promise spiritual wealth to those who follow Him.

1. Peter says we are to arm ourselves with the same attitude as Christ, who suffered in His body. What attitude is Peter talking about? How do you arm yourself with a similar attitude? Can you claim to live in victory with that same attitude as Christ?

2. Peter called his readers to use their spiritual gifts to serve others. How do you use your spiritual gifts? Do you seek to administer God's grace to those who are lot, hurting, or in need?

1 Peter 5

BACKGROUND

Peter refers to Jesus as the Chief Shepherd. Jesus is referred to as a shepherd elsewhere in the New Testament. References include: Good Shepherd (Jn. 10.11.14), Great Shepherd (Heb. 13.20), and Shepherd and Overseer (1 Pet. 2.25).

In Peter's time, Rome was referred to as Babylon not only in Jewish literature but in Roman literature as well. By the first century, the Babylon of the Old Testament had become an insignificant town.

OVERVIEW

Though Peter had the privilege of knowing Christ personally and could rightfully claim to be an apostle, he viewed himself on the same level as others who provided leadership to the church.

Peter stipulated five attitudes and responsibilities elders have when they lead the body of Christ:

- *Shepherd the flock*—lead, protect, guide, and feed

- *Overseer*—ensuring members are cared for and living according to God's Word
- *Willingly*—serving joyfully rather than out of duty
- *Eagerly*—motivated by growth in those they oversee rather than personal, monetary gain
- *Example*—not only preach the life of Christ but personally live it

Those who adhere to the stipulations listed above and serve God faithfully will receive an eternal reward.

Young people are to be respectful of those who lead the church. Peter stated that God would exalt those who are humble when He deems it appropriate. God cares for His people and will see that their needs are cared for.

Sober means to be self-disciplined, while *vigilant* means to be alert. Both are required to avoid the pitfalls Satan tries to place before believers to make them stumble. As an enemy, Satan is *always* employing hostilities and accusations to make God's people fall. The only way to avoid such pitfalls is to resist in determined and resolute faith. Since all believers experience Satan's attacks, individuals experiencing spiritual attack can take comfort from and find courage in knowing they are not alone.

Peter prayed for God to work in four ways in the lives of those who experience suffering and Satan's attacks:

- *Perfect*—mend and return to a state of wholeness
- *Establish*—stability in the believer's faith walk
- *Strengthen*—fortify and build up
- *Settle*—God's foundation that makes believers steadfast and secure

Silas is referred to repeatedly in Acts in association with both Peter and Paul. Silvanus is his Aramaic name (Acts 15:22, 27, 32, 34, 40; 16:19, 25, 29; 17:4, 10, 14-15; 18:5).

She is thought to refer either to Peter's wife, who is known to have traveled with him (1 Cor. 9.5), or the body of believers in Rome.

Mark refers to Peter's spiritual son, John Mark.

INSIGHTS

In the 1970s, comedian Flip Wilson popularized the phrase *the devil made me do it*. Today, some radical preachers want to place the sole blame for sin on Satan. Yet what Peter told his readers 2,000 years ago is still true today. Believers can and should resist the temptations of Satan. Because believers belong to God, Satan cannot possess them and, therefore, cannot *make* them do anything. However, he is crafty and cunning and will use all of his resources to present us with temptations that we find exceedingly hard to resist. With God, there is *always* a way to resist (1 Cor. 10.13). If we ask, God will give us His strength to overcome.

1. Peter suggested humility is something believers can put on. How do you do so? How can humility be the root of all you do? How can your respond to others with humility? Who proves most challenging to remaining humble as you interact with others? Do you ask God for His strength to do what you struggle with?

2. How do you see the devil prowling around and waiting to devour whomever he can? How can you be self-controlled and alert to the devils tactics? How does knowing others suffer at the hands of the devil give you strength in your own suffering? What are some means of standing firm in faith that help you resist the devil?

SECOND PETER

While the motivation for writing his first letter came from the external persecution suffered by many Christians, Peter's reason for writing his second letter came from the proliferation of false teachings within the church. Peter reminded his readers that the Christian life required diligence in pursuing all the characteristics that conformed one into the image of Christ. The false teachers, on the other hand, displayed many characteristics that were contrary to the Christian life: arrogance, greed, covetousness, and a lack of appreciation for the coming judgment. Peter urged his readers to live godly, blameless lives as a means of combating the false teachings.

There is a definite similarity between 2 Peter and Jude. It was a common practice in the first century to borrow material from other sources. Some scholars believe the more refined language in Jude suggests that Peter borrowed from Jude's letter. It is also possible that both authors borrowed from a third source that has not survived.

Second Peter can be divided into three parts along chapter lines. The first exhorts readers to pursue Christian character and spiritual maturity. The second condemns false teachers while the third encourages believers to look with confidence to the hope of Christ's return.

2 Peter 1

BACKGROUND

In ancient times, *tent* was a common metaphor for the body. The metaphor pointed to the temporary nature of the body.

Peter had been told by Jesus that he would be taken captive and put to death (Jn. 21.18-19).

OVERVIEW

Peter began his letter by pointing out the invaluable gift each believer possessed: precious faith.

Peter used a standard greeting to open his letter. *Grace and peace* combined Greek and Hebrew salutations. In joining these salutations with the *knowledge of God and . . . Jesus*, Peter suggested that the salutations are more than a greeting. They are blessings that come from faith in Christ.

Peter used the phrase *great and precious promises* to refer to the many statements of divine provision found throughout the scriptures.

Peter's list of qualities that believers are to pursue build upon each other. Virtue is the same word Peter used in reference to Christ's character (v. 3). It is obtained through obedience to God's Word.

By being diligent in obtaining these qualities, the believer would lead the fruitful and productive life God had equipped and gifted each to live. A lack of these qualities indicates that a believer was focused on the things of the earth rather than spiritual realities. Such a focus leads to an inability to see God's work and a failure to remember the cleansing work of Christ's death and resurrection.

The evidence of God's presence (*call and election*) in a believer's life is continuing spiritual growth and maturity. By diligently seeking the qualities Peter listed, a believer would be sure of growth (*be fruitful*), would not stumble, and would enjoy the abundant blessing of everlasting life.

Peter understood the necessity of remembering God's truths and wrote three times of his desire to remind his readers about them.

Some false teachers claimed that Jesus' resurrection and second coming were cleverly conceived stories that had no basis in reality. Peter testified to his own eyewitness of the Transfiguration (Matt 17.1-8) as proof of the reality of these truths.

For those who might doubt Peter's testimony,

even stronger confirmation of the truth exists—the prophecies of the Old Testament, which find their fulfillment in the life, death, and resurrection of Christ. Such fulfilled prophecies should be heeded because they cast a light into the darkness and will continue to do so until the morning star appears, i.e., until Christ's return.

The Greek word for *interpretation* can also mean *origin*. The Greek context makes it clear that Peter was stating that no person could claim to have originated the scriptures. All of scripture comes from God. Even the prophets who spoke on God's behalf did not invent their messages but delivered their various accounts in obedience to the prompting of the Holy Spirit.

INSIGHTS

Peter's list of faith, virtue, knowledge, self-control, perseverance, godliness, brotherly kindness, and love are worth pursuing today. The one way of guaranteeing a life of worth, fruitfulness, and fulfillment is to actively engage in the ways of God. Peter's list provides a tremendous foundation for doing just that.

1. Peter reminded his readers that God called them by His glory and virtue and had given great and precious promises. Can you name some of the things God has promised us as believers? Do you view the promises as precious? What can you do to gain more understanding of and hope in the promises of God?

2. Peter listed a progression of qualities that grow one on another. Do you make an effort to increase these qualities in your life? Have you seen how they can keep you from being ineffective and unproductive in your knowledge of Christ? How are these qualities able to help protect you from falling prey to the false teachings and lies of the world?

2 Peter 2

BACKGROUND

Balaam was more interested in what he could get than in speaking God's truth. He hoped to gain monetary payment from a pagan for cursing Israel. So unattuned was he to God's ways that his donkey was able to see what he could not—God's angel standing in the road with his sword drawn (Num. 22-24).

Peter's reference to a pig returning to the mud came from an extra-biblical source (the story of Ahiqar) with which his readers would have been familiar.

OVERVIEW

Having established at the end of the last chapter that God's Word comes only from God, Peter described false teachers whose instruction was contrary to the truth.

In Peter's estimation, false teachers were akin to the false prophets of the Old Testament. The difference in terms suggests the teachers of Peter's time were distorting the scriptures rather than claiming to be prophets who had heard from God, as in the Old Testament.

False teachers readily took advantage of their followers in order to realize personal gain. Though their judgment and destruction may not be apparent, it will eventually come to pass.

Peter used three examples to show that God's judgment would come upon those who were distorting His Word: the angels who followed Satan when he rebelled against God (Rev. 12.4), the people of Noah's time who were judged by the flood (Gen. 6-9), and the people of Sodom and Gomorrah who were judged for their wicked ways (Gen. 19.1-29). The last two events in particular illustrate God's protection upon those who follow after Him even when the surrounding society has fallen into great immorality.

Noah was called a *preacher of righteousness* because of his obedience to God and the opportunity he had to speak the truth as he built the ark.

Three times Lot is referred to as righteous. Though Lot appears to be influenced by worldly values in the Genesis account, Peter states that God rewarded Lot because of his refusal to be influenced by the immoral standards that surrounded him.

Peter compared those who disregarded God to wild beasts. They lived only in their present reality and had no ability to consider the consequences of their actions. Those who live only for personal pleasure will eventually find that pleasure has caused their demise.

Though pagans often participated in drunken revelries, those who did so during the daytime were viewed with disdain. Likewise, false teachers who shared their lies in the light of Christian truth were not only viewed with disdain but would eventually be met with judgment.

Peter compared false teachers to wells that contained no water or clouds that produced no rain. The flawed expectations of false teachers would be just as disappointing.

False teachers used natural human sexual inclinations to lure believers back into the bondage of sin. False teachers promised great freedom, though they themselves were in the throes of sin.

Peter does not clearly define the *they* he used beginning in verse 20. Whether it refers to false teachers or those led astray, his point is that those who know God's truth but fail to obey it will experience God's judgment.

INSIGHTS

Knowing God's truth is not enough; failing to put it into practice is disobedience. God does not want the world simply to know *about* Him. He wants the world to experience the joy, freedom, and protection that come from being obedient to Him. As a result, obedience is much more highly valued than knowledge.

1. Peter paints a very bleak future for those who chose not to believe and chose to intentionally blaspheme God. Do you take the opportunities God gives you to share His truth with those who are misinformed and/or do not know the love, mercy, and justness of God? Do you pray regularly for those who are far from God?

2. Peter writes that those who believe in Christ and then later follow the ways of the world are worse off than those who never believed in the first place. What are you doing to ensure you don't fall prey to the deception and lies of the world? Are you reading scripture daily and meeting with other believers regularly?

2 Peter 3

BACKGROUND

Whether the first letter to which Peter refers is the letter today known as 1 Peter is uncertain. First Peter was addressed to churches in five provinces (1 Pet.1.1), whereas 2 Peter appears to be addressed to a single church or small group of churches. Also, 1 Peter does not appear to be a reminder letter as Peter states in his second letter (2 Pet. 3.1). As a result, some believe another letter that has not survived was written to this same group of believers.

OVERVIEW

False teachers tended to play down the second coming of Christ and future judgment. Peter reminded his readers of the reality of these two events and the necessity to prepare for them.

False teachings could be recognized and exposed by comparing their teachings to the teachings of the prophets and the apostles.

One motivation for living a righteous life is to prepare for the second coming of Christ. Peter warned that the delay in Christ's return would lead some to scoff at the notion and rationalize that nothing had changed since the beginning of time.

The fathers who fell asleep refer to the Old Testament patriarchs.

Peter contends that some people have forgotten the everlasting quality of God's Word. His Word formed the earth and heavens. His Word caused the flood that destroyed the earth. His Word restored the earth after the flood. His Word allows the earth to continue until the time of judgment (at Christ's second coming). God has all things under His control.

Though Christ *seemed* to be delayed in returning as promised, Peter reminded his readers that God does not count time in the same manner humans do. What might seem to believers like a long time is very short in God's scheme of things. One reason for Christ's delay is to allow as many people as possible to hear God's Word and choose to believe. In that way, more people will have the opportunity to spend eternity with God than if Christ returned more quickly.

The day of the Lord is an Old Testament phrase that refers to the end times and God's final judgment. Only God knows when this final judgment will take place (Mark 13.32-35). The earth and all that is in it will be completely destroyed. One of the great hopes believers have is that the corrupted earth will be replaced by Christ's eternal reign on a new earth.

While false teachers minimize the future judgment and, therefore, live in whatever manner they choose, believers know the judgment will occur and should be motivated by it to live in a manner pleasing to God.

Peter equated Paul's writings with scripture, in effect confirming that Paul wrote the Word of God.

Untaught refers to those who are untrained in disciplines of the mind. *Unstable* refers to those who choose to be disobedient to God's Word.

Peter encouraged his readers to resist the false teachings because they knew the truth. Instead, they were to grow in the grace and knowledge of Christ.

INSIGHTS

It is interesting to note that Peter stated Paul's writings on the end times were hard to understand—comfort for believers today who may have trouble interpreting his writings!

Today, those who do not believe in Christ have just as much reason to scoff at Christ's return as did the people of Peter's time. Christ's return has been delayed by almost 2,000 years, which some take to mean He will not be returning at all. Despite unbelievers' rationalizing, believers can take comfort in the truth of God's Word. More and more events and statements in the Bible are being confirmed by archeological evidence and other findings. Things once thought impossible to have occurred have been confirmed. God's Word is true and believers can have confidence that what God says will happen will actually come to pass.

1. Peter was engaged in correspondence with his readers in order to encourage them in the truths they had learned. Who are you engaging with, whether believer or unbeliever, in order to remind them of and encourage them to grow in the truths of God? If you are not engaged with anyone, who might God be calling you to enter into relationship with for this purpose?

2. Peter reminded his readers that they had heard the same things from Paul, who had also written to them. Do you look for opportunities to build up and commend other people as they engage in ministry? Do you strive to be united with other believers?

JUDE

Jude, the half brother of Jesus and full brother of James (Mk. 6.3), wrote this short epistle to sound a warning against the false teachers and thinking that were distorting the truth of Christ. Jude was passionate about his belief in Christ and encouraged his readers to recognize and speak against those who did not share the same faith or tried to twist its meaning. Jude's use of groups of three throughout the book is worth noting and was designed to add emphasis to his message.

There is a definite similarity between Jude and 2 Peter. It would seem a certainty that one author borrowed from the other, though who borrowed from whom is uncertain. Some scholars point to the anticipation in 2 Peter and the apparent past tense of Jude's writing to argue that Peter wrote first. Other scholars argue that the more precise language found in Jude means it was written first. Still other scholars believe both Peter and Jude borrowed from a third, unknown author.

JUDE

BACKGROUND

The Assumption of Moses is an apocryphal book, which is purported to contain the final instructions of Moses to Joshua. The book also contains a passage in which Michael and Satan dispute over Moses' body.

Enoch, the great-grandfather of Noah, is purported to have written *1 Enoch,* an extra-biblical book. It is included in the canonical scriptures of the Ethiopian Orthodox Church but not of any other Christian church. Jude's use of the content from these books does not suggest he believed these texts were inspired.

OVERVIEW

Jude had intended to write a general letter that focused on the salvation he and his readers found in Christ. However, doctrinal error had crept into the church and required more immediate attention.

Those who teach that *saved by grace* means one can live any way one chooses perverts God's gift of grace.

Jude used three Old Testament examples to show God judges those who choose to do wrong:

- God delivered His people out of Egyptian bondage but later judged those who disobeyed His ways (Ex. 13- 14; 32).
- The angels who rebelled against God will one day be judged.
- The inhabitants of Sodom and Gomorrah engaged in all kinds of perverted sexual acts (strange flesh means homosexuality) resulting in destruction of both them and their cities (Gen. 19).

The ungodly men were called *dreamers* because either their *gods* were the product of their imagination or their denial of Christ meant they were living in an unreal world.

Those who did not speak the truth were compared to three Old Testament characters who opposed God: Cain killed his brother (Gen. 4.3-8), Balaam tried to profit from doing the work of God (Num. 22-24), and Korah challenged those God had placed in authority (Num. 16).

The Greek word translated as *spot* can also be translated as *hidden reefs* or *blemishes*. It warned the readers to be on guard against anything that spoiled or brought deception into their understanding and celebration of God's truth.

Love feasts referred to the early church's celebration of the Lord's Supper.

Jude's quote from *1 Enoch* includes four uses of *ungodly* to drive home the point that God will judge those who are wicked in nature and do evil.

Grumblers and complainers were those who misused their words to dissuade people from following the truth of God and instead follow their own selfish and enslaving reality.

Jude reminded his readers that Jesus had warned against the false teachers who would appear and attempt to cause believers to disavow their faith. As such, these heretics should not take anyone by surprise. They should, instead, be expected and actively guarded against.

INSIGHTS

Jude's encouragement to keep within the love of God is well worth heeding today. God will never withdraw His love from us as long as we are not in a state of deliberate and prolonged rebellion against Him. We can avoid the temptation to turn our backs on God, as well as to participate in many sinful activities by pursuing God's love. This can be done in a variety of ways including regularly reading His Word and thereby getting to know God more intimately, being obedient to His commandments and will for our lives, praying, and quieting ourselves before Him in order to hear Him speak to us.

1. How do you build yourself up in the faith? Do you pray in the Holy Spirit? As you live out your faith in a community of believers, how do you protect against those who would come to divide by relying on their own instincts rather than God's truth?

2. What does it mean to contend for the faith? How do you steward the truths entrusted to you as a believer? How can we work together to guard against those who would creep into our midst to twist, distort, and deny the truths of God?

Acknowledgements

There are an amazing number of people who are involved in a project like this. First, my thanks go to Dave Wood for asking me to write a series of New and Old Testament notes to accompany our church's Bible reading program. Dave saw something in me that I did not see. As a result I had the privilege and blessing of seeing God's hand work in and through me in most unexpected ways.

Thanks also go to the leadership and staff of Grace Community Church, in particular Bryan Hochhalter, Doug Kempton, Bryce Gray, Paula Smith, Tracey Krusz, and others who worked behind the scenes.

Thank you to Eddie Jones and Lighthouse Publishing of the Carolinas. Eddie's vision for my manuscript and belief in what I had written has been an enormous encouragement and beyond that, has resulted in a published work – a dream come true!

Thank you to Meaghan Burnett who walked me through the entire publication process. I've had to step way out of my comfort zone in some areas. Thank you for your patience, explanations, training and efforts on my behalf.

A myriad of people helped with readying the manuscript for publication. These include Peggy Bennett, Stacey and Martin Bilderbeck, Heather Brdak, Kristine Bresser, Vito Ciaravino, Luke Elliott, Dick Klemisch, Jennifer Matous, Diane Matous, Tom Reisner, Karen Straetmans, Dawn Taylor, and Ally Turner. Thank you for the gift of your time and effort. I appreciate each of you immensely.

With so many people involved right up to the day the books are printed, I am sure I have overlooked someone who rightly deserves to be listed here. Please know this is an oversight. My gratitude goes to you as well!

I could not have finished this project without my husband, Phil. His love, support, encouragement and belief in me have been amazing. More than once I have been overwhelmed with the amount of work needed to complete this series. Each time Phil has reminded me of who I am, whose I am, and the real author and finisher of this work. I love you!!

Finally and most importantly, thank you God! You have shown me incredible grace and mercy, gifted me in ways I never would have guessed, been gentle in Your rebukes and showered me with Your blessings. Praise be to You, God our Father and our Lord Jesus Christ!!

Made in the USA
San Bernardino, CA
29 May 2016